Generative AI and Quantum Computing: A Practical Guide

Contents

Part I: Foundations

Chapter 1: Introduction to Generative AI

Overview of Generative AI

Generative AI refers to a class of artificial intelligence systems capable of creating new content by learning patterns from existing data. Unlike traditional AI systems that focus on recognizing patterns and making predictions, generative AI generates data similar to what it has been trained on.

Key Concepts

- **Generative Models**: Algorithms that learn the underlying structure of a dataset to generate new, similar data.
- **Training Data**: The dataset used to train the model.
- **Generated Output**: New data produced by the model, such as text, images, or audio.

Example: Text Generation

Consider a generative AI model trained on a collection of Shakespearean plays. The model learns the style, language, and structure of the text, allowing it to generate new sentences in the style of Shakespeare.

python

Copy code

```python
# Example code using GPT-3 for text generation
import openai

openai.api_key = 'your-api-key'

prompt = "Write a sonnet in the style of Shakespeare"
response = openai.Completion.create(
    engine="davinci",
    prompt=prompt,
    max_tokens=100
)
```

```
print(response.choices[0].text.strip())
```

Applications and Impact

- **Creative Writing**: AI-generated stories, poems, and scripts.
- **Art**: Creation of paintings, music, and digital art.
- **Business**: Automated content creation, personalized marketing materials.
- **Healthcare**: Drug discovery, medical imaging analysis.

Historical Context and Evolution

The development of generative AI has evolved significantly over the decades:

- **1950s**: Early AI experiments with simple rule-based systems.
- **1980s**: Introduction of neural networks.
- **2010s**: Emergence of deep learning and significant advancements in generative models.
- **Present**: Advanced models like GPT-3, DALL-E, and StyleGAN demonstrating high-quality generation capabilities.

Fundamentals of Quantum Mechanics

Quantum mechanics is the foundation of quantum computing, dealing with phenomena at atomic and subatomic levels. Key principles include:

- **Superposition**: Quantum bits (qubits) can exist in multiple states simultaneously.
- **Entanglement**: Qubits can be correlated in such a way that the state of one qubit can depend on the state of another, even at a distance.
- **Interference**: Quantum states can interfere with each other, leading to constructive or destructive interference.

Quantum Bits and Quantum States

Qubits

A qubit is the basic unit of quantum information, analogous to a bit in classical computing but with quantum properties.

- **Classical Bit**: Can be 0 or 1.
- **Qubit**: Can be in a state |0>, |1>, or any superposition $\alpha|0> + \beta|1>$, where α and β are complex numbers.

Example: Qubit Representation

A qubit can be represented on the Bloch sphere, where any point on the sphere represents a possible state of the qubit.

Quantum Gates and Circuits

Quantum gates manipulate qubits and are the building blocks of quantum circuits. Common quantum gates include:

- **Pauli-X Gate**: Flips the state of a qubit.
- **Hadamard Gate**: Creates a superposition state.
- **CNOT Gate**: Entangles two qubits.

Example: Quantum Circuit

python

Copy code

```python
# Example code using Qiskit to create a simple quantum circuit

from qiskit import QuantumCircuit, Aer, execute


# Create a quantum circuit with one qubit

qc = QuantumCircuit(1)


# Apply a Hadamard gate to put the qubit in superposition

qc.h(0)


# Execute the circuit on a quantum simulator

backend = Aer.get_backend('statevector_simulator')

result = execute(qc, backend).result()

statevector = result.get_statevector()


print(statevector)
```

Types of Generative Models

1. **Autoencoders**: Learn to compress data into a lower-dimensional space and then reconstruct it.

2. **Variational Autoencoders (VAEs)**: Probabilistic approach to autoencoders with continuous latent variables.

3. **Generative Adversarial Networks (GANs)**: Consist of a generator and a discriminator in a game-theoretic framework

4. **Normalizing Flows**: Transform simple probability distributions into more complex ones.

5. **Energy-Based Models**: Learn the energy landscape of the data distribution.

Example: VAE

python

Copy code

Example code for a simple VAE using TensorFlow/Keras

```python
from tensorflow.keras.layers import Input, Dense, Lambda

from tensorflow.keras.models import Model

from tensorflow.keras.losses import mse

import tensorflow as tf


# Encoder

input_data = Input(shape=(784,))

encoded = Dense(64, activation='relu')(input_data)

z_mean = Dense(2)(encoded)

z_log_var = Dense(2)(encoded)


# Sampling function

def sampling(args):

    z_mean, z_log_var = args

    batch = tf.shape(z_mean)[0]

    dim = tf.shape(z_mean)[1]

    epsilon = tf.keras.backend.random_normal(shape=(batch, dim))

    return z_mean + tf.keras.backend.exp(0.5 * z_log_var) * epsilon
```

```python
z = Lambda(sampling, output_shape=(2,))([z_mean, z_log_var])


# Decoder

decoder_input = Input(shape=(2,))

decoded = Dense(64, activation='relu')(decoder_input)

output_data = Dense(784, activation='sigmoid')(decoded)


# Models

encoder = Model(input_data, [z_mean, z_log_var, z])

decoder = Model(decoder_input, output_data)

output_combined = decoder(encoder(input_data)[2])

vae = Model(input_data, output_combined)


# Loss function

reconstruction_loss = mse(input_data, output_combined) * 784

kl_loss = 1 + z_log_var - tf.square(z_mean) - tf.exp(z_log_var)

kl_loss = tf.reduce_mean(kl_loss) * -0.5
```

```python
vae_loss = tf.reduce_mean(reconstruction_loss + kl_loss)

vae.add_loss(vae_loss)
vae.compile(optimizer='adam')

# Example data (use MNIST dataset for training in practice)
import numpy as np
x_train = np.random.rand(1000, 784)
vae.fit(x_train, epochs=10, batch_size=32)
```

Mathematical Foundations

Generative models are often based on probabilistic frameworks, involving concepts such as probability distributions, latent variables, and Bayesian inference.

Key Concepts

- **Latent Variables**: Hidden variables that capture the underlying structure of the data.

- **Probability Distributions**: Mathematical functions that describe the likelihood of different outcomes.

Key Algorithms and Techniques

1. **Maximum Likelihood Estimation (MLE)**: A method for estimating the parameters of a statistical model.

2. **Bayesian Inference**: A probabilistic approach to inference and learning.

3. **Gradient Descent**: An optimization algorithm for finding the minimum of a function.

Example: Gradient Descent

python

Copy code

```
# Example code for gradient descent optimization

import numpy as np


# Objective function: f(x) = x^2
```

```python
def f(x):

    return x**2


# Derivative of the objective function: f'(x) = 2x

def df(x):

    return 2 * x


# Gradient descent algorithm

x = 10  # Initial guess

learning_rate = 0.1

num_iterations = 100


for i in range(num_iterations):

    x = x - learning_rate * df(x)

    print(f"Iteration {i+1}: x = {x}, f(x) = {f(x)}")
```

This content provides a foundational understanding of generative AI and quantum computing, including practical examples, code snippets and explanations of key concepts.

Quantum Algorithms Overview

Quantum algorithms leverage the principles of quantum mechanics to solve problems more efficiently than classical algorithms. Key quantum algorithms include:

- **Shor's Algorithm**: For integer factorization.

- **Grover's Algorithm**: For unstructured search.

- **Quantum Fourier Transform**: Foundation for many quantum algorithms.

- **Variational Quantum Eigensolver (VQE)**: For solving optimization problems.

- **Quantum Approximate Optimization Algorithm (QAOA)**: For combinatorial optimization.

Shor's Algorithm

Overview

Shor's algorithm efficiently factors large integers, a task that is computationally intensive for classical computers. This algorithm ha significant implications for cryptography.

Steps

1. **Quantum Fourier Transform**: Used to find the periodicity in a function.

2. **Modular Exponentiation**: Key step to find the period of a function related to the integer to be factored.

3. **Classical Post-processing**: Extracts the factors from the period found by the quantum part.

Example Code

Here's an outline using Qiskit for a simplified version of Shor's algorithm:

python

Copy code

```
# Import necessary libraries
```

```python
from qiskit import QuantumCircuit, Aer, execute

from qiskit.visualization import plot_histogram


# Define parameters

n = 15  # The number to be factored

a = 7   # A random number less than n


# Create a quantum circuit with 8 qubits and 8 classical bits

qc = QuantumCircuit(8, 8)


# Apply Hadamard gates to the first 4 qubits

for i in range(4):

    qc.h(i)


# Apply controlled-U gates (simplified for this example)

for i in range(4):

    qc.cx(i, i + 4)
```

```python
# Apply the inverse Quantum Fourier Transform

for i in range(4):

    qc.h(i)

    for j in range(i):

        qc.cu1(-np.pi / float(2 ** (i - j)), j, i)


# Measure the first 4 qubits

for i in range(4):

    qc.measure(i, i)


# Execute the quantum circuit

backend = Aer.get_backend('qasm_simulator')

result = execute(qc, backend).result()

counts = result.get_counts()


# Plot the result

plot_histogram(counts)
```

Use Cases and Impact

Shor's algorithm can potentially break RSA encryption, which relies on the difficulty of factoring large numbers. This has profound implications for data security and encryption.

Grover's Algorithm

Overview

Grover's algorithm searches an unsorted database with NNN entries in $O(N)O(\sqrt{N})O(N)$ time, offering a quadratic speedup over classical search algorithms.

Steps

1. **Initialization**: Prepare a superposition of all possible states.

2. **Oracle**: Marks the correct solution by flipping its phase.

3. **Amplitude Amplification**: Increases the probability amplitude of the correct solution.

Example Code

Here's an implementation using Qiskit:

python

Copy code

```python
# Import necessary libraries

from qiskit import QuantumCircuit, Aer, execute

from qiskit.visualization import plot_histogram


# Create a quantum circuit with 2 qubits and 2 classical bits

qc = QuantumCircuit(2, 2)


# Apply Hadamard gates to both qubits

qc.h([0, 1])


# Oracle for marking the solution (01 in this example)

qc.cz(0, 1)


# Apply Hadamard gates to both qubits again

qc.h([0, 1])
```

```python
# Measure both qubits

qc.measure([0, 1], [0, 1])


# Execute the quantum circuit

backend = Aer.get_backend('qasm_simulator')

result = execute(qc, backend).result()

counts = result.get_counts()


# Plot the result

plot_histogram(counts)
```

Use Cases and Impact

Grover's algorithm is useful for searching large unsorted databases and has applications in cryptography, optimization, and database search.

Quantum-enhanced Machine Learning

Quantum machine learning aims to enhance classical machine learning algorithms by leveraging quantum computing's unique capabilities.

Key Concepts

- **Quantum Data**: Data stored in quantum states.
- **Quantum Models**: Machine learning models implemented on quantum computers.
- **Quantum Speedup**: Potential acceleration of learning and inference processes.

Quantum Data and Quantum Models

Quantum data refers to information represented in quantum states. Quantum models leverage quantum circuits and gates to process thi data.

Example: Quantum Support Vector Machine (QSVM)

QSVM uses quantum circuits to perform kernel evaluations more efficiently.

python

Copy code

```python
# Import necessary libraries
from qiskit import QuantumCircuit, Aer, execute
from qiskit.aqua.algorithms import QSVM


# Define training data
training_data = {'A': [[1, 0]], 'B': [[0, 1]]}
test_data = {'A': [[0.8, 0.2]], 'B': [[0.2, 0.8]]}


# Create a quantum SVM instance
qsvm = QSVM(training_data, test_data)


# Execute the QSVM algorithm
```

```
backend = Aer.get_backend('qasm_simulator')

result = qsvm.run(backend)


# Print the classification results

print(result['testing_accuracy'])
```

Case Studies

- **Quantum-Enhanced Neural Networks**: Hybrid models

  combining classical neural networks with quantum layers.

- **Quantum Reinforcement Learning**: Quantum circuits for state

  representation and action selection in reinforcement learning

Variational Quantum Eigensolver (VQE)

VQE is used for finding the ground state energy of a quantum system, which can be applied to optimization problems.

Example Code

python

Copy code

```
# Import necessary libraries
from qiskit import Aer
from qiskit.circuit.library import RealAmplitudes
from qiskit.algorithms import VQE
from qiskit.opflow import PauliSumOp


# Define the Hamiltonian of the system
H = PauliSumOp.from_list([("Z", 1)])
```

```python
# Define the variational ansatz

ansatz = RealAmplitudes(1)


# Create a VQE instance

vqe = VQE(ansatz, optimizer='SPSA',

quantum_instance=Aer.get_backend('statevector_simulator')


# Execute the VQE algorithm

result = vqe.compute_minimum_eigenvalue(H)


# Print the result

print("Minimum eigenvalue:", result.eigenvalue.real)
```

Quantum Boltzmann Machines

Quantum Boltzmann Machines (QBM) are used for modeling probability distributions.

Example Code

```python
# Import necessary libraries

from qiskit import Aer

from qiskit.aqua.algorithms import QBM


# Define the training data

training_data = np.array([[1, 0], [0, 1], [1, 1], [0, 0]])


# Create a QBM instance

qbm = QBM(training_data, num_qubits=2,

quantum_instance=Aer.get_backend('qasm_simulator'))


# Train the QBM

qbm.train()


# Print the trained parameters

print("Trained parameters:", qbm.params)
```

Quantum Generative Adversarial Networks (QGANs)

QGANs combine quantum generators and discriminators to generate data.

Example Code

python

Copy code

```
# Import necessary libraries
from qiskit import Aer
from qiskit.machine_learning import QGAN
from qiskit.circuit.library import TwoLocal


# Define the training data
training_data = np.random.rand(100, 1)


# Define the quantum generator ansatz
generator_ansatz = TwoLocal(1, 'ry', 'cz', reps=1)
```

```python
# Create a QGAN instance

qgan = QGAN(training_data, generator_ansatz,

quantum_instance=Aer.get_backend('statevector_simulator'))


# Train the QGAN

qgan.train()


# Generate new data

generated_data =

qgan.generator.generator.run(qgan.generator.generator.initial_poin

t)


# Print the generated data

print("Generated data:", generated_data)
```

These sections provide an in-depth look at quantum computing

algorithms and their intersection with generative AI, including

practical examples, use cases, and hands-on exercises.

Quantum Speedup in AI

Quantum speedup refers to the ability of quantum computers to solve certain problems faster than classical computers. In AI, this speedup can be particularly valuable for tasks such as optimization, sampling, and machine learning model training.

Example: Quantum Speedup in Optimization

Quantum algorithms like the Quantum Approximate Optimization Algorithm (QAOA) can solve combinatorial optimization problems more efficiently than classical algorithms.

python

Copy code

```
# Import necessary libraries
from qiskit import Aer, QuantumCircuit
from qiskit.circuit.library import QAOAAnsatz
from qiskit.algorithms import QAOA
```

```python
from qiskit.opflow import PauliSumOp

from qiskit.optimization.applications.ising.max_cut import

get_operator


# Define the Max-Cut problem graph

w = [[0, 1, 1], [1, 0, 1], [1, 1, 0]]


# Get the QAOA operator

qubit_op, offset = get_operator(w)


# Define the QAOA ansatz

p = 1

qaoa_ansatz = QAOAAnsatz(qubit_op, p=p)


# Create a QAOA instance

qaoa =

QAOA(quantum_instance=Aer.get_backend('statevector_simulator'))
```

```python
# Find the optimal parameters

result = qaoa.compute_minimum_eigenvalue(qubit_op)


# Print the results

print("Optimal parameters:", result.optimal_point)

print("Optimal value:", result.optimal_value)
```

Practical Implementations

Integrating quantum computing into AI systems involves using quantum algorithms to enhance classical AI methods. This can be done through hybrid quantum-classical models.

Example: Hybrid Quantum-Classical Neural Network

In a hybrid model, quantum circuits are used as layers within classica neural networks to improve computational efficiency.

python

Copy code

```python
# Import necessary libraries
```

```python
from qiskit import QuantumCircuit, Aer

from qiskit.utils import QuantumInstance

from qiskit_machine_learning.algorithms.classifiers import VQC

from qiskit_machine_learning.circuit.library import

RawFeatureVector


# Define the quantum instance

quantum_instance =

QuantumInstance(Aer.get_backend('statevector_simulator'))


# Define the feature map and variational form

feature_map = RawFeatureVector(4)

var_form = QuantumCircuit(4)


# Create a VQC instance

vqc = VQC(feature_map, var_form,

quantum_instance=quantum_instance)
```

```python
# Define training data

X_train = np.array([[0, 1, 0, 1], [1, 0, 1, 0]])

y_train = np.array([0, 1])


# Train the VQC

vqc.fit(X_train, y_train)


# Print the accuracy

print("Training accuracy:", vqc.score(X_train, y_train))
```

Challenges and Limitations

While quantum computing offers significant potential, there are

challenges and limitations:

- **Noise**: Quantum computers are susceptible to errors due to

  environmental interference.

- **Scalability**: Current quantum systems have a limited number o

  qubits.

- **Resource Requirements**: Quantum algorithms require substantial computational resources.

Chapter 8: Hybrid Quantum-Classical Systems

Integration of Classical and Quantum Systems

Hybrid quantum-classical systems combine the strengths of both paradigms, using quantum processors for specific tasks while leveraging classical processors for others.

Example: Quantum Kernel Estimation

Quantum kernel methods use quantum circuits to estimate kernel functions, enhancing classical support vector machines (SVM).

python

Copy code

```
# Import necessary libraries

from qiskit import Aer
```

```python
from qiskit.circuit.library import ZZFeatureMap

from qiskit_machine_learning.kernels import QuantumKernel

from qiskit_machine_learning.algorithms.classifiers import QSVC


# Define the feature map

feature_map = ZZFeatureMap(feature_dimension=2, reps=2)


# Define the quantum kernel

quantum_instance = Aer.get_backend('statevector_simulator')

quantum_kernel = QuantumKernel(feature_map=feature_map,

quantum_instance=quantum_instance)


# Create a QSVC instance

qsvc = QSVC(quantum_kernel=quantum_kernel)


# Define training data

X_train = np.array([[0, 1], [1, 0]])

y_train = np.array([0, 1])
```

```
# Train the QSVC

qsvc.fit(X_train, y_train)


# Print the accuracy

print("Training accuracy:", qsvc.score(X_train, y_train))
```

Algorithms and Architectures

Hybrid architectures involve integrating quantum circuits into classical machine learning models. Examples include hybrid neural networks and quantum-assisted optimization algorithms.

Use Cases

- **Quantum Chemistry**: Hybrid models simulate molecular structures more efficiently.

- **Financial Modeling**: Quantum algorithms enhance risk analysis and portfolio optimization.

Quantum Optimization Algorithms

Quantum optimization algorithms solve complex optimization problems by leveraging quantum parallelism and entanglement.

Example: Quantum Approximate Optimization Algorithm (QAOA)

QAOA is used for solving combinatorial optimization problems such as the Max-Cut problem.

python

Copy code

```
# Import necessary libraries
from qiskit import Aer
from qiskit.circuit.library import QAOAAnsatz
from qiskit.algorithms import QAOA
from qiskit.opflow import PauliSumOp
from qiskit.optimization.applications.ising.max_cut import get_operator
```

```python
# Define the Max-Cut problem graph

w = [[0, 1, 1], [1, 0, 1], [1, 1, 0]]


# Get the QAOA operator

qubit_op, offset = get_operator(w)


# Define the QAOA ansatz

p = 1

qaoa_ansatz = QAOAAnsatz(qubit_op, p=p)


# Create a QAOA instance

qaoa =

QAOA(quantum_instance=Aer.get_backend('statevector_simulator')


# Find the optimal parameters

result = qaoa.compute_minimum_eigenvalue(qubit_op)
```

```
# Print the results
print("Optimal parameters:", result.optimal_point)
print("Optimal value:", result.optimal_value)
```

Real-world Applications

- **Supply Chain Optimization**: Quantum algorithms optimize logistics and inventory management.
- **Energy Management**: Quantum optimization improves energy distribution and consumption.

Comparative Analysis

Quantum optimization algorithms offer potential speedup over classical methods, but practical implementation requires addressing noise and error correction.

Quantum Cryptography

Quantum cryptography leverages quantum mechanics principles to enhance security, particularly through Quantum Key Distribution (QKD).

Example: Quantum Key Distribution

QKD uses quantum states to securely distribute cryptographic keys.

python

Copy code

```
# Import necessary libraries

from qiskit import QuantumCircuit, Aer

from qiskit.visualization import plot_histogram


# Define the quantum circuit for QKD

qc = QuantumCircuit(2, 2)
```

```python
# Apply Hadamard gates to both qubits

qc.h([0, 1])


# Measure both qubits

qc.measure([0, 1], [0, 1])


# Execute the quantum circuit

backend = Aer.get_backend('qasm_simulator')

result = execute(qc, backend).result()

counts = result.get_counts()


# Plot the result

plot_histogram(counts)
```

Implications for AI Security

Quantum AI enhances security in machine learning models by

leveraging quantum encryption and secure communication protocols.

Future Prospects

- **Post-Quantum Cryptography**: Developing cryptographic algorithms resistant to quantum attacks.

- **Quantum Secure Machine Learning**: Ensuring the integrity and confidentiality of AI models in a quantum future.

These sections provide a comprehensive understanding of quantum computing for AI acceleration, including practical implementations, challenges, hybrid systems, optimization, and security considerations. Each topic includes examples, code, and hands-on exercises to enhance learning.

Part IV: Practical Implementation and Future Directions

Overview of Quantum Programming Languages

Quantum programming languages are designed to express quantum algorithms and control quantum computers. The most popular languages include:

- **Qiskit**: An open-source SDK for working with quantum computers, developed by IBM.
- **Cirq**: A Python library for designing, simulating, and running quantum circuits on Google's quantum processors.
- **PyQuil**: A library for quantum programming using Quil, developed by Rigetti.
- **Q#**: A quantum programming language developed by Microsoft as part of the Quantum Development Kit.

Each language offers unique features and is often associated with a specific quantum computing platform.

Practical Coding Examples

Qiskit Example: Creating a Quantum Circuit

python

Copy code

```python
from qiskit import QuantumCircuit, Aer, execute

# Create a Quantum Circuit with 2 qubits and 2 classical bits
qc = QuantumCircuit(2, 2)

# Apply a Hadamard gate to the first qubit
qc.h(0)

# Apply a CNOT gate with control qubit 0 and target qubit 1
qc.cx(0, 1)

# Measure both qubits
qc.measure([0, 1], [0, 1])

# Execute the circuit on the qasm simulator
```

```
backend = Aer.get_backend('qasm_simulator')

result = execute(qc, backend).result()

counts = result.get_counts(qc)


print("Measurement outcomes:", counts)
```

Tools and Libraries

- **Qiskit**: Provides tools for creating quantum circuits, running them on simulators, and on real quantum computers.
- **Cirq**: Focuses on creating, editing, and invoking quantum circuits and providing a platform for running them.
- **PyQuil**: Integrates with the Quil programming language and provides tools for creating quantum programs and running them on Rigetti's quantum processors.
- **Q#**: Part of the Microsoft Quantum Development Kit, designed for writing, testing, and running quantum algorithms.

Example: Using Cirq to Simulate a Quantum Circuit

```python
import cirq


# Create two qubits
qubit_0, qubit_1 = cirq.LineQubit.range(2)


# Create a circuit
circuit = cirq.Circuit(
    cirq.H(qubit_0),            # Apply Hadamard gate to qubit 0
    cirq.CX(qubit_0, qubit_1),  # Apply CNOT gate with qubit 0 as
control and qubit 1 as target
    cirq.measure(qubit_0),      # Measure qubit 0
    cirq.measure(qubit_1)       # Measure qubit 1
)


# Simulate the circuit
simulator = cirq.Simulator()
```

```
result = simulator.run(circuit, repetitions=1000)


print("Measurement results:")

print(result)
```

Chapter 12: Building Quantum Generative Models

Step-by-Step Implementation

Example: Variational Quantum Eigensolver (VQE) with Qiskit

python

Copy code

```python
from qiskit import Aer, QuantumCircuit

from qiskit.algorithms import VQE

from qiskit.circuit.library import TwoLocal

from qiskit.opflow import PauliSumOp


# Define the Hamiltonian (example: H = Z)

H = PauliSumOp.from_list([("Z", 1)])


# Define the ansatz

ansatz = TwoLocal(rotation_blocks='ry', entanglement_blocks='cz'


# Create a VQE instance

vqe = VQE(ansatz, optimizer='SPSA',

quantum_instance=Aer.get_backend('statevector_simulator'))
```

```
# Execute the VQE algorithm

result = vqe.compute_minimum_eigenvalue(H)


print("Minimum eigenvalue:", result.eigenvalue.real)
```

Real-world Case Studies

Case Study: Quantum Generative Adversarial Networks (QGANs)

- **Scenario**: A financial institution uses QGANs to generate realistic financial data for stress testing.
- **Approach**: They implement QGANs using Qiskit to learn from historical data and generate new scenarios.
- **Outcome**: Improved accuracy in stress testing models, leading to better risk management strategies.

Performance Evaluation

Performance evaluation of quantum generative models involves comparing their accuracy, efficiency, and scalability against classical models. Key metrics include:

- **Accuracy**: How closely the generated data matches real-world data.

- **Efficiency**: The computational resources required.

- **Scalability**: The ability to handle larger datasets and more complex models.

Case Study 1: Accelerating Drug Discovery with Quantum-Enhanced Generative Models

Objective:

To explore how combining generative AI with quantum computing can accelerate drug discovery by rapidly generating molecular structures that meet specific pharmacological criteria.

Overview:

This case study describes a project where quantum computers are leveraged to perform complex molecular simulations, reducing the time and computational resources required in drug design. Traditional generative AI models, such as Variational Autoencoders (VAEs) or Generative Adversarial Networks (GANs), generate candidate molecules, while quantum computing refines these molecules by simulating their properties and interactions.

Key Components:

1. **Data Preparation** – Utilizing databases of molecular structures, pharmacokinetics, and binding affinities.

2. **Quantum Optimization** – Using quantum-enhanced

   optimization for simulating quantum states and predicting

   binding efficiencies.

3. **AI Model Integration** – Applying GANs to generate molecular

   structures that quantum computers further analyze for

   potential as drug candidates.

Outcomes:

This fusion of technologies yields accelerated discovery times and

increases the probability of finding effective drug compounds. It

demonstrates the effectiveness of generative AI and quantum

optimization in producing viable drugs more quickly than traditional

methods.

Case Study 2: Optimizing Supply Chain Logistics with Quantum-Inspired Generative Models

Objective:

To use generative AI and quantum computing to optimize supply chain routes, predict demand fluctuations, and suggest efficient logistical solutions in real time.

Overview:

This case examines how a retail company facing challenges in supply chain efficiency utilized generative AI to create demand predictions and logistical models. By leveraging quantum computing's optimization capabilities, the company refined these models to produce cost-effective and time-efficient solutions.

Key Components:

1. **Data Integration** – Real-time data from inventory, customer orders, and transportation logistics.

2. **Demand Prediction** – Employing AI to generate demand forecasts based on seasonal, regional, and economic factors.

3. **Quantum Optimization Algorithms** – Enhancing AI prediction with quantum algorithms to suggest optimal transportation routes and inventory management.

Outcomes:

This hybrid approach led to significant reductions in operational costs, improved delivery times, and reduced environmental impact. The study highlights the potential of quantum computing in streamlining large-scale logistical challenges.

Case Study 3: Financial Fraud Detection Using Quantum-Supported Generative AI

Objective:

To detect and prevent financial fraud by utilizing generative AI to model potential fraudulent behaviors and quantum computing to analyze these patterns at scale.

Overview:

This case follows a financial institution that incorporated generative AI models to create synthetic profiles of fraudulent transactions. Quantum computing enhances these models by processing and analyzing transaction data with high-dimensional correlations that are otherwise challenging to detect with classical computing.

Key Components:

1. **Data Collection** – Compiling large datasets of transaction histories, customer profiles, and known fraud cases.

2. **Generative AI Simulation** – Modeling potential fraudulent activities through GANs to create synthetic fraud scenarios.

3. **Quantum Analysis** – Using quantum computing to identify hidden patterns and interdependencies within the synthetic data that may suggest real fraud risks.

Outcomes:

The project resulted in early and accurate fraud detection, reducing financial losses and improving customer trust. This case illustrates the advantages of using generative models for synthetic data generation and quantum computing for uncovering complex, nuanced patterns.

Case Study 4: Climate Modeling and Prediction Using Quantum-Assisted Generative AI

Objective:

To advance climate change models by combining generative AI's data generation capabilities with quantum computing's complex processing power to produce accurate, granular predictions.

Overview:

This case study focuses on a research initiative to develop highly detailed climate models, generating various weather and environmental scenarios using generative AI. Quantum computing enables the handling of complex interactions within these models, such as atmospheric dynamics and oceanic flows, for more precise climate forecasts.

Key Components:

1. **Environmental Data Sourcing** – Aggregating global data on weather, atmospheric conditions, and emissions.

2. **Scenario Generation** – Using generative AI to produce potential

   climate scenarios under different environmental policies.

3. **Quantum Simulation** – Simulating the interactions in these

   models on a quantum computer, capturing details that improve

   prediction accuracy.

Outcomes:

This approach offers robust climate models capable of projecting

potential climate changes and assisting policymakers in identifying

impactful interventions. The case underlines the potential for

quantum-assisted generative models in addressing complex

environmental issues.

Case Study 5: Enhancing Creative Content Generation with Quantum Computing and Generative AI

Objective:

To utilize quantum computing and generative AI for creative applications, such as generating original music, art, and design, by exploring new patterns and styles.

Overview:

This case covers a project in the entertainment industry where generative AI models generate initial content, like music or artwork, while quantum computing introduces creative variations based on complex data manipulation. Quantum algorithms can suggest novel style combinations, chord progressions, and color palettes that generative AI alone might not produce.

Key Components:

1. **Content Dataset** – Extensive datasets on existing art styles, music genres, and design elements.

2. **Generative AI Models** – Creating initial content using models like GANs and VAEs to emulate human creativity.

3. **Quantum-Enhanced Creativity** – Applying quantum algorithms to introduce novel variations, enabling more unpredictable and diverse creative outputs.

Outcomes:

The result is a variety of innovative content that attracts audiences with unique, engaging forms of art and music. This case demonstrates the capacity of quantum computing to enhance the creative potential of generative AI.

Case Study 6: Optimizing Renewable Energy Grids with Quantum-Inspired Generative Models

Objective:

To develop a hybrid approach using generative AI and quantum computing for optimizing energy distribution in renewable energy grids, aiming to minimize energy loss and balance supply with fluctuating demand.

Overview:

This case study focuses on how an energy provider used generative AI models to simulate energy consumption patterns and quantum computing to optimize the flow of energy from renewable sources, such as solar and wind. Quantum optimization helps tackle the complex challenges of managing energy distribution dynamically across various regions and times, given the variability in renewable sources.

Key Components:

1. **Data Gathering and Pattern Recognition** – Collecting data on weather conditions, energy production from renewables, and historical usage patterns.

2. **Generative AI for Demand Forecasting** – Generating demand forecasts that account for daily and seasonal changes in energy consumption.

3. **Quantum Optimization for Grid Balancing** – Using quantum algorithms to optimize energy flow, reducing losses by adjusting distribution to match real-time demand closely.

Outcomes:

The project led to increased energy efficiency, better integration of renewable sources, and a reduction in grid maintenance costs. This case demonstrates how generative AI combined with quantum computing can support sustainable energy management and optimize the use of renewable resources.

Case Study 7: Personalized Healthcare Treatment Planning with Quantum-Assisted Generative Models

Objective:

To enhance treatment planning by creating personalized healthcare solutions based on patient data and condition-specific treatment models, using quantum computing to analyze complex biological data.

Overview:

This case study explores how a healthcare provider developed personalized treatment plans by using generative AI to create tailored medical scenarios. Quantum computing further refines these scenarios by analyzing genomic, metabolic, and lifestyle data, leading to highly individualized treatment plans. This approach addresses the challenge of providing effective treatment recommendations for patients with unique genetic and health backgrounds.

Key Components:

1. **Data Integration and Preprocessing** – Collecting patient-specific data, including genomics, medical history, and lifestyle factors.

2. **Generative AI for Scenario Generation** – Using models to simulate possible treatment outcomes based on varying medical interventions.

3. **Quantum Analysis for Precision Medicine** – Applying quantum computing to process and analyze high-dimensional patient data, identifying optimized treatments with the highest potential for success.

Outcomes:

The project enabled healthcare providers to deliver more precise and effective treatments, reducing trial-and-error approaches and improving patient outcomes. This case highlights the potential for quantum-assisted generative models in personalized medicine, providing a pathway for precision treatments in complex medical cases.

Case Study 8: Advanced Material Design for Sustainable Manufacturing Using Quantum and Generative AI

Objective:

To design new, sustainable materials with specific properties (such as durability, biodegradability, and lightweight strength) for manufacturing, using generative AI to propose material compositions and quantum computing to test and refine these designs.

Overview:

This study details an initiative where a manufacturing company leveraged generative AI to propose innovative material compositions, followed by quantum simulations to predict material properties and interactions. Quantum computing allows for the simulation of atomic and molecular structures, leading to an accelerated discovery of sustainable materials that can replace traditional, resource-intensive materials.

Key Components:

1. **Data Preparation and Input** – Analyzing existing materials with

   desired properties, like strength, flexibility, and sustainability.

2. **Generative AI for Material Design** – Proposing new material

   structures by combining known elements and generating

   potential material compounds.

3. **Quantum Simulation for Material Testing** – Using quantum

   computing to model the molecular structure and predict

   performance in different conditions, identifying materials with

   optimal properties.

Outcomes:

This approach resulted in the development of new, sustainable

materials that reduced environmental impact and manufacturing

costs. It showcases how generative AI and quantum computing

together can revolutionize material science, offering a pathway

toward eco-friendly and innovative materials in manufacturing.

Ethical Considerations in Quantum AI

Quantum AI introduces new ethical considerations, including:

- **Data Privacy**: Ensuring the privacy of data used in quantum machine learning.
- **Algorithmic Bias**: Addressing bias in quantum algorithms to ensure fair outcomes.
- **Security**: Ensuring robust security measures to protect against quantum attacks.

Societal Impact

Quantum AI has the potential to transform various industries, but it also raises societal concerns:

- **Job Displacement**: Automation of complex tasks could lead to job losses.

- **Inequality**: Access to quantum computing resources could widen the gap between tech-advanced and less-advanced regions.
- **Ethical AI**: Ensuring that AI developed using quantum computing adheres to ethical guidelines.

Future Ethical Challenges

Future challenges include:

- **Regulatory Frameworks**: Developing regulations for the ethical use of quantum AI.
- **Transparency**: Ensuring transparency in how quantum AI models are trained and used.
- **Accountability**: Establishing accountability for decisions made by quantum AI systems.

Emerging Trends

- **Quantum Advantage**: Identifying specific problems where quantum computers outperform classical counterparts.
- **Integration**: Seamless integration of quantum and classical computing resources.
- **Hybrid Algorithms**: Development of hybrid algorithms that leverage both quantum and classical strengths.

Long-term Prospects

- **Scalability**: Increasing the number of qubits and improving error correction techniques.
- **Accessibility**: Making quantum computing more accessible to developers and researchers.
- **Applications**: Expanding the range of applications for quantum AI in fields like healthcare, finance, and logistics.

Vision for the Future

The future of generative AI and quantum computing promises:

- **Revolutionary Advancements**: Transformative changes in computational capabilities.
- **New Paradigms**: Emergence of new computational paradigms and problem-solving approaches.
- **Ethical AI**: Development of ethical frameworks to guide the responsible use of quantum AI technologies.

These sections provide a comprehensive overview of practical implementations, ethical considerations, and future directions in quantum computing and generative AI. Each topic includes detailed explanations, practical examples, and hands-on exercises to facilitate learning and application.

www.ingramcontent.com/pod-product-compliance
Lightning Source LLC
LaVergne TN
LVHW051609050326
832903LV00033B/4416